GREAT
TRUCKS

GREAT
TRUCKS

JOHN CARROLL

Chelsea House Publishers
Philadelphia

Published in 1998 by
Chelsea House Publishers
1974 Sproul Road, Suite 400, P.O. Box 914
Broomall, PA 19008-0914

Library of Congress Cataloging-in-Publication Data applied for

ISBN 0-7910-4998-1

Printed in China

JOHN CARROLL is a full-time motoring
journalist who has written books and
contributed to magazines on numerous
subjects, including cars and motorcycles.
This book of trucks from around the world
is a labour of love as he has been fascinated
with them from an early age.

**PHOTOGRAPHS SUPPLIED BY
ANDREW MORLAND**

TITLE PAGE: A Freightliner wrecker truck
BELOW: A Kenworth cab.
RIGHT: A cabover Freightliner.

Contents

INTRODUCTION

Trucks are a phenomenon of the 20th century. They evolved from the horse-drawn wagons of the last years of the 19th century and have subsequently developed into the highly complex machines that, apart from having wheels and carrying loads, bear little resemblance to their predecessors. The earliest trucks were little more than horse-drawn machines equipped with engines powered by steam, petrol or diesel; but the modern truck is indispensable to life on planet earth as we know it today.

Trucks are used to move goods on every continent, in every country and by every type of organization. They are fundamental to the economy of nations as well as to their security, trucks being a vital component of every army's equipment. Trucks have also influenced the development of countries by reason of their important role in commerce and construction.

As trucks have advanced and evolved designers have geared them to more specialized roles: trucks to cross rough terrain, trucks to haul enormous loads on surfaced roads, others designed for military applications, for construction and forestry and yet others for firefighting and more. It is no exaggeration to say that the list is endless.

The type of terrain on which trucks are put to work affects their design; the huge open spaces and interstates of North America have prompted the development of the 'eighteen-wheeler', Australia has room for 'road trains' while the 'cabover' design of tractor unit can be seen as more appropriate to crowded European roads.

The following chapters take an encyclopedic look at many of the great truck marques from around the world.

ABOVE LEFT

Ford's Model AA truck was mass-produced as a general medium-weight truck from the Twenties onwards. It is based on Ford's cab of the time but note that the AA truck has dual rear tyres and heavy duty rims to increase its payload.

ABOVE

Atkinson and Maudslay were two English truck manufacturers who made cab over engine trucks such as the L1586 (left) of 1944 and the Mogul Mk II (right) of 1946 of which these are preserved examples. In the later postwar years, both firms were absorbed by other truck manufacturers.

American trucks are massive as witnessed by this 1980 Peterbilt eighteen-wheeler. It is known as a 'conventional' design because the cab is not positioned over the engine. Peterbilt is currently part of the Paccar group of companies.

CHAPTER ONE
THE EARLY DAYS

It is generally acknowledged that the era of mechanically propelled transport started in 1769 when Nicholas Cugnot built a three-wheeled vehicle with steam propulsion capable of 4 mph. It ran in the streets of Paris and was designed to carry four passengers. A Welsh inventor, Oliver Evans, who had emigrated to America and lived in Maryland produced a elementary steam wagon in 1772. He examined the possibilities of applying steam power to propel a vehicle and in 1787 was granted the right to manufacture a steam wagon in the United States. His wagon never made it as far as production but he did build a steam-powered dredging machine that he rigged to drive from its place of manufacture to the River Schuylkill before being driven to Delaware.

In 1788, a vehicle built along similar lines – the Fourness – was built in Great Britain. By 1831 the idea was proven and men such as Sir Charles Dance and Walter Hancock operated a number of steam coaches on regular routes. The latter's machines were capable of up to 20 mph. The railway age boomed but the mechanization of road transport was a natural progression and experimentation towards practical methods of implementation continued in both Europe and the United States.

In the closing years of the 19th century, internal combustion-engine-powered vehicles began to make an appearance and names like Benz, Daimler, De Dion, Panhard and Peugeot became prominent in Europe, while in Britain, Albion, Dennis, Humber, Napier, Sunbeam and Wolseley became widely known.

The first British commercial vehicle that was both viable and practical was made by Thornycroft in 1896. That same year, the crippling 'Red Flag Act' was repealed which had previously forced the operators of vehicles powered by the internal combustion engine to employ a man to walk before them with a warning flag. Tthe repeal of this odd legislation paved the way for the development of road transport in the United Kingdom.

A year earlier, Richard F. Stewart of Pocantico Hills, New York, produced a truck with a 2-hp Daimler engine and internal gear drive and two years later began to produce trucks for sale. These were steam-powered with a marine-type steam boiler and vertical engine.

Within a few years Thorneycroft had produced the world's first articulated truck. The British Army was quick to realize its potential and by 1899 had purchased some for use in

Foden, based in Cheshire, England, successfully produced steam trucks until 1929 when it made the decision to concentrate entirely on diesel-engined truck production. This steam wagon,

'Queen Mary', was built in 1908 and was supplied to an English brewery company.

Bean produced trucks of a conventional design alongside those of many other manufacturers as road haulage in the U.K. established itself.

The Ford Model T was truly a milestone in motoring history: it was cheap and one of the first vehicles to bring mobility to the masses. It was inevitable that its makers would produce commercial variants such as this 1-ton van of 1923.

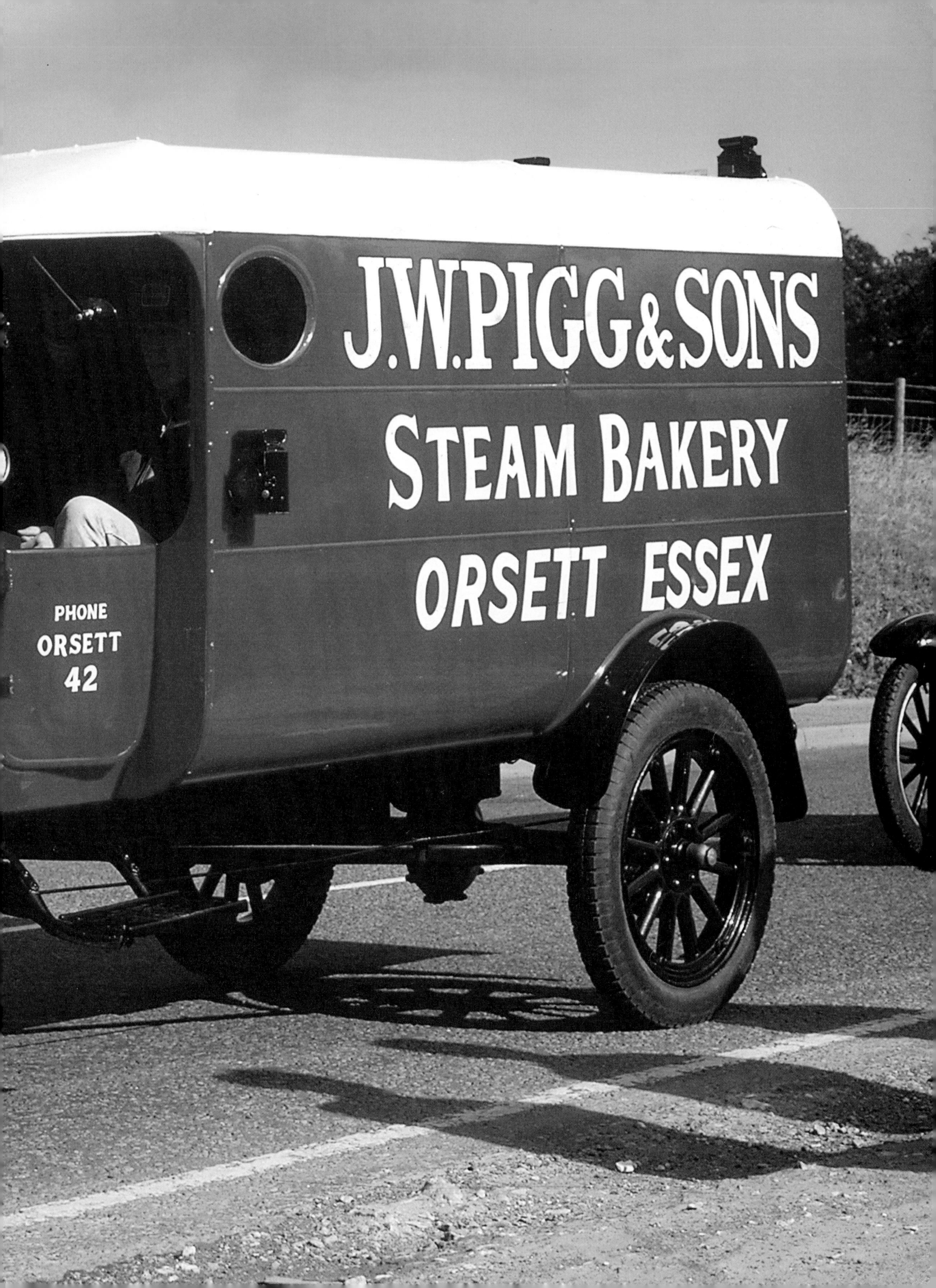
J.W.PIGG & SONS
STEAM BAKERY
ORSETT ESSEX
PHONE
ORSETT
42

Foden was one of the last of the British manufacturers to produce steam-powered vehicles such as this one from 1932 which was relatively sophisticated and featured pneumatic front tyres. The company did, however, shift to diesel truck manufacture.

the Boer War in South Africa. Leyland vehicles appeared in 1896 under the auspices of the Lancashire Steam Motor Company whose first vehicle was a van with an oil-fired boiler and two-cylinder compound engine. Manufacturers of steam traction engines began to build steam lorries and one of them, Foden, was to become the world's largest maker of steam vehicles.

In 1897 the Daimler Motor Company of Coventry, England, offered a petrol-engined commercial vehicle. It was designed by Panhard and powered by a Daimler internal combustion engine. From this they went on to build other similar machines.

Across the Atlantic the first Mack truck was rolling out of the Brooklyn works. The company had been established by five brothers of German parentage who had formerly operated a Brooklyn smithy. The smithy was gradually turned over to the production of trucks and their first is reputed to have travelled a million miles. In 1904 the brothers built a charabanc which they named the Manhattan and by 1905 had been sufficiently successful to be able to transfer their operation to Allentown, Pennsylvania where they introduced the Model AC. This was the truck that earned them the 'Bulldog' Mack nickname. It was a four-cylinder petrol-engined truck based on a pressed steel chassis frame. Transmission was by means of a three-speed gearbox through a jackshaft which had chain drive to the rear wheels which were fitted with solid tyres. The truck featured a cab, which was unusual at the time, and was of a bonneted type. The AC was supplied in significant numbers to the British Army in France where it earned the Bulldog tag. Another landmark from Mack was the predecessor of the 'cab over engine'

design when it was realized that if the driver sat over the engine it was possible to incorporate a longer load bed in a chassis of the same length. The fledgeling Mack company also developed the Junior model, a 2-ton truck intended for lighter duties which in many ways was the forerunner of the delivery van.

In the early 1900s came the realization that both the public as well as potential customers needed

educating in the advantages of commercial truck manufacture and a series of trials was organized known as The Liverpool Trials. They were run in 1898, 1899 and 1901 for steam-powered vehicles. The Automobile Club of America organized similar events based on the success of certain French trials of 1897. The American trials were two-day events and featured classes for steam-, petrol- and electric-powered machines. The outcome was

that the internal combustion-engined truck carried the honours. A more practical test was organized for 1904 when for five days the trials simulated actual working conditions with employees of the American and Weskit Express Companies taking part. Trucks were a relatively common sight by 1904, especially in the .5- to 3-ton capacity. Larger trucks tended to be steam-powered.

By 1910, numerous ideas for trucks

and their design had been tried and some were rejected, such as rear-engined belt-driven machines. The popular configuration was proving to be front-engined with either forward or normal control depending on the position of the driver's seat and steering wheel. Proving the trucks was a recurrent theme: a Swiss-designed Saurer, built in Plainfield, New Jersey, undertook a journey from Denver, Colorado to New York. Other

Ford held a strong share of the new truck market in the mid-Fifties when they produced this truck. Its styling was clearly recognizable right across the range to the famous F-100 pickup. This particular model has a considerably greater payload than the smaller F-100 and is of a cabover design.

manufacturers followed these enterprising examples. In 1912, trucks made by FWD, White and Autocar travelled 1500 miles through the southern states in 45 days averaging 33 miles per day. This was far faster than the pack mules previously employed despite dreadful road surfaces.

Tyres were a component that required attention: the pneumatic tyre had been introduced by the Michelin brothers in 1895 but a suitable truck tyre still remained to be developed. By 1919 most trucks in the United States of up to two tons were so equipped.

Further progress was made in Germany at Maschinenfabrik Augsburg-Nürnberg (MAN) when the first successful diesel engine was produced. The engine, of a compression ignition type, is accepted as the invention of Doctor Rudolf Diesel. Improvements continued apace as both steam- and internal combustion-engined vehicles became more refined and newer manufacturers began to make their presence felt, such as Commer, Crossley, Morris and Standard in Britain. In the United States early manufacturers included Pierce-Arrow, Oldsmobile and the McCormick Harvesting Machine Company which later became International Harvester. The founder of Oldsmobile, Ransom E. Olds, later went on to form Reo. Passenger-carrying companies used vehicles that were still known as omnibuses and were becoming increasingly reliant on petrol-engined vehicles. In London, the London General Omnibus Company started its own manufacturing and repair operations which led to the success of the AEC, the Associated Engineering Company. In 1916 a company known as the Gerlinger Motor Car Company was founded in Portland, Oregan. It went into liquidation in 1917 but was purchased by two men in 1923. Their names were Kent and Worthington and the new venture, Kenworth, was an amalgamation of their surnames.

The British Army was still using steam-engined lorries but in the first decade of the 20th century was becoming increasingly interested in the motor lorry which resulted in the establishment of the War Office subsidy scheme. This required truck manufacturers to build to a standard specification. The purchasers of such trucks were paid a subsidy to encourage them to maintain their vehicles in first class condition so that, in the event of war, the War Office could purchase them back immediately. War broke out in Europe in 1914 and the policy paid dividends. A similar scheme was initiated in Germany where it was known as the *Leichter Armee Lastzug* and a third similar scheme in France. The Americans were slower to employ

trucks for military service, possibly because they were not being subjected to the same degree of international tension as the Europeans at that time.

Nevertheless, it was a military expedition that proved the worth of motorized vehicles to the U.S. Army, the expedition in question being that of General Pershing into Mexico in 1916. Soon after, trucks from White, Autocar, FWD and Mack became standard U.S. Army equipment. The American manufacturers, especially Mack and FWD, were also supplying their products to the Allied Armies in Europe. From these humble beginnings

military thinking turned towards the production of tanks and of personnel carriers after a number of London buses were successfully used to transport British soldiers up to the front during the war.

In the Twenties, the British market was flooded with cheap army surplus trucks readily available to individuals in need of transport facilities. This heralded the establishment of specialist hauliers with fleets of trucks offering their services to manufacturers. Many army surplus vehicles were converted into what became known as

charabancs. These were usually open-topped vehicles with rows of seats for passengers and became popular as a way of transporting ordinary people on days out and ultimately led to the development of another off-shoot – the motor coach. Malcolm Loughhead patented the four wheel hydraulic braking system as the 'Lockheed' in 1919. The same year Goodyear and Dunlop announced pneumatic tyres.

A decline in the use of petrol engines followed as diesels became more developed. MAN had the first major success with this form of engine when its four-cylinder units were ordered by the Bavarian Post Office

after it was exhibited at the 1924 Berlin Motor Show. In Britain, Mercedes and Saurer diesel-engined trucks were in use on the roads by 1930. British manufacturers were not slow to emulate the type and two famous companies were established in this decade – Gardner and Perkins. In France, too, diesel made an appearance with the Morton engine of 1929. Across the Atlantic, Kenworth was the first American manufacturer to install diesel engines in its trucks which it did from 1932 onwards. The cheapness of petrol in the United States and the less punitive taxes meant that the trend towards diesel was less quickly established although, ultimately, trucks went diesel there too. The stage was set for the rapid development of trucks into the highly technical machines of the second half of the 20th century.

Fargo was another American manufacturer of commercial vehicles and produced this 1-ton truck in 1930.

CHAPTER TWO
GREAT AMERICAN TRUCKS

The large eighteen-wheeler American type is what usually springs to mind when the word truck is mentioned. It is easy to imagine the bonneted Bulldog Mack on a freeway somewhere, silhouetted against a sunset. The reality and the myth aren't too far apart as jukeboxes in a thousand truckstop diners testify. *'Let me tell you a story about a man we all know ... Truck-driving outlaw where d'ya go? He drives a semi ... truck driving outlaw ... He drives from coast to coast to satisfy his soul, the things that keep him going are to hear those big wheels roll ... truck-driving outlaw ...'*
This is one of the many songs dedicated to the men regarded by many as the modern counterparts of cowboys, hobos and frontiersman.

What is really surprising about interstate trucking is just how recently it has evolved into the form in which it exists today. The truckstop started to appear in the Forties as trucks came to rely on diesel fuel. This was not available at normal gas stations so special places sprang up to service the trucks. The freeway construction programme and establishment of companies who could haul goods all over continental America, such as Pacific Intermountain Express, in a professional way, and running to a time-table, established the industry.

The distances are enormous, coast-to-coast is a three-day run, drivers stopping only for food and fuel. The glamour is there but so are the seedier aspects – drivers working excessive hours, driving defective trucks in order to meet schedules and deliveries, less than equitable practices involving teamsters, unions and the itinerant labour that often unloads trucks for cash payments – it is all there beneath the romance.

As in other countries the truck industry started with any number of tiny companies producing trucks. Rapid was based in Detroit, Michigan as was Grabowsky. Knox, Wisconsin Duplex, Walker and Sterling were four more manufacturers that were in business prior to the Twenties but, unlike Mack, FWD and Autocar did not survive for long.

Chevrolet

As part of General Motors Corporation (GMC), Chevrolet has manufactured numerous trucks throughout its history. It produced many trucks for the allied cause during World War II – in fact, it was the main supplier of 1.5-ton 4x4 trucks to the U.S. Army at that time. These trucks were of a standardized design powered by a six-in-line petrol

Many truckers spend thousands of hours and dollars personalizing the truck in which they spend their days on the road. An example of the kind of work carried out is this customized Kenworth.

engine, driving through a four-speed transmission and two-speed transfer case. The chassis was of a steel ladder-type with leaf sprung suspension. A steel closed cab of the conventional design and a cargo rear body and canvas tilt completed the NJ-G-7107, as it was tagged. Chevrolet of Canada also produced trucks for the Allies including the C30 and the 1311X3.

By the mid-Sixties, Chevrolet was producing a number of medium-weight trucks as well as the tractor units for semi-trailers, including the HM 70000 4x2 tractor and its stablemate the Series JJ 70000, a 6x4 tractor unit. The medium-weight trucks included the Series L 50 and Series N 50, conventional and cabover trucks respectively. More recently, Chevrolet

has produced trucks such as the C60, a medium-weight tractor unit of the conventional design available with a choice of engines including petrol or Detroit or Caterpillar diesels. Badge engineering means that certain Chevrolet trucks appear as GMCs and even Isuzus.

Diamond Reo

Diamond Reo Trucks was formed in

1967 after the amalgamation of the two companies – Diamond T and Reo Motors Incorporated who were at the time both constituent parts of the White Motor Corporation. White had acquired Diamond T in 1958 for $10 million. In 1970 they produced the CO-7864D, the tractor for a typical eighteen-wheeler of its day. The tractor unit was powered by a 212-bhp

Cummins NH220 six-cylinder diesel which drove through a Spicer five-speed gearbox to a tandem-drive rear bogie which had dual tyres on each axle end. It was a cabover design with a semi-trailer coupling over the rear bogie.

Freightliner

Freightliner sold out to Daimler-Benz in 1983. The price paid by the

ABOVE LEFT
A Watkins Motor Lines cabover Diamond Reo refuelling in Lakeland, Florida.

ABOVE
A late-Seventies cabover GMC Astro 95 operated by Allied Van Lines. This truck was sold with a choice of transmissions and either Detroit or Cummins diesels.

European manufacturer is reported to have been $260 million! Freightliner made its name on the strength of the FLC 1200 series that it introduced in 1979. These fuel-efficient trucks proved viable in the fuel crisis of 1980 and Freightliner has built on this success with a series of aerodynamically shaped trucks that are even more fuel efficient as well as wind-tunnel tested.

GMC

This massive corporation started in a small way. In 1903, William C. Durant took control of Buick and in 1908 founded the General Motors Company which absorbed a number of early car and truck makers. In 1911 the truck names were changed to GMC who acquired Chevrolet during World War I. Another merger followed in 1925 and another in 1943, each time increasing in size. General Motors Corporation now has interests in many companies around the globe. In terms of truck manufacture its most important are Vauxhall, formerly Bedford in the U.K., Opel in Germany, Chevrolet and GMC in the U.S.A. and Isuzu in Japan. There are also considerable numbers of other companies in which it has an interest. Many of its products are lightweight commercial vans and delivery trucks but the GMC Astro and General models are heavyweight American trucks par excellence. The three-axle GMC General of the late Eighties is a bonneted design and under this feature is found a variety of big diesel

engines including the Detroit, Cummins and Caterpillar which have outputs ranging between 268 and 470 bhp. Transmissions, too, are complex and massive – up to 15 forward gears can be selected. The General will pull up to 65 tons gross combined weight (of trailer and tractor unit). The three-axle GMC Astro is a cabover design but comes with a similarly bewildering choice of engines and transmissions. The sleeper cab tilts to allow engine access and the tractor

unit will cope with a gross combined weight of up to 45 tons.

International

Truck manufacturer International was part of a major agricultural engineering group that was split up in the Eighties. In 1986 it became Navistar International although its products are still known as Internationals. The American-made International 9370 is a 6x4 conventional available with a range of proprietary engine and transmission options such as Detroit diesel engines.

Kenworth

This company was originally founded in 1916 as the Gerlinger Motor Company and specialized in trucks for the logging industry. In recent years it became part of the Paccar Group which also owns Peterbilt. Towards the end of the Seventies its range consisted of the C500, K100 and Super 953 models. Within each of these designations is a range of models. The C500 models, for example, are heavy duty trucks fitted with the equipment for specialized operations such as earth moving, logging and mixing. As well as specifying the body type the customer could choose between Detroit, Caterpillar and Cummins engines. In the K100 trucks both normal control and cabover models were manufactured as the tractor units for semi-trailers. The Super 953 models are monstrous six-wheel-drive oilfield trucks used off-highway for large scale projects.

This 1974 Kenworth conventional was photographed in Nevada where it was being used to haul vegetables. It has a sleeper cab fitted to enable its drivers to rest along the way when travelling coast-to-coast.

Mack

Mack was one of the pioneers of American truck manufacture having commenced production in 1900. The company expanded after introducing its famous range of trucks – the nickname 'Bulldog' Mack enduring to this day. The AC4 of 1919 was one of the most famous of the Bulldog range – the numerical suffix denoting a four-cylinder engine as there was also a six,

the AC6. The AC4 produced 75 bhp and featured a four-speed transmission. The whole truck was based around a steel channel chassis and leaf sprung suspension. In the Seventies the company produced its F-Series of tractor units for road use. These were 6x4 trucks of a cabover design. The sleeper cab made them suitable for long haul American trucking and the truck was powered by a 672-cubic inch six-

cylinder diesel that produced 302 bhp. The transmission featured seven forward and five reverse gears.

Oshkosh

This company was founded in 1917 by William R. Besserlich and Bernard A. Mosling in Oshkosh, Wisconsin, to produce all-wheel-drive trucks for use on unsurfaced routes and in winter conditions. Their first production truck was the Model A and was powered by a

Herschel-Spillman four-cylinder engine and four-wheel-drive. The company sold only 23 vehicles in 1924 but sold many more of the new Model H introduced in 1925. It became established as the basis for road construction and snow-plough trucks. In 1930 the company produced the world's first pneumatic-tyred earth mover. The trucks from this Wisconsin firm soon earned a good reputation as

dependable hard working machines and their cross-country performance meant that they found favour in the timber and similar industries. Specialist oil drilling, firefighting and heavy haulage trucks are now produced by the company as well as an 8x8 HEMTT for the U.S. Army. These initials stand for Heavy Expanded Mobility Tactical Truck and it is suited to a number of heavy haulage roles for the U.S. Army.

Bulldog is the nickname earned by Mack trucks which is one of the oldest American truck makers. Seen here (above left) are a row of bonneted U607T models, the cabs of which are made of fibreglass. As well as specialist trucks for logging and similar operations, Mack also makes conventional trucks for interstate haulage such as (above) this early-Eighties tractor unit. Note the Bulldog hood ornament.

ABOVE

Peterbilt produced the 353 models in the early Eighties as both 6x4 and 6x6 rigids for tough conditions. They have steel and aluminium cabs. The body fitted to this one, photographed in California, is for loose loads such as earth that can be dumped from the hydraulically lifted load bed.

Paccar

This conglomerate developed from companies with long-standing involvement in truck manufacture. Its American truck brands are Peterbilt and Kenworth of which in excess of 10,000 trucks of each are built per annum. In Mexico, Kenmex is part of the Paccar group which is an acronym for Pacific Car and Foundry. In Europe Paccar owns Foden which it acquired in 1980. A Paccar plant also produces trucks in Australia.

Peterbilt

While this company is now part of the Paccar group, it still produces vehicles badged as Peterbilt trucks. One such is the Peterbilt 349, a heavy duty truck for on and off highway use. It is supplied as a three-axle chassis cab with a range of optional engines and is designed so that the operator can install a rear body to turn it into a transit mixer, a salt tipper or snow plough – all can be fitted. The cab is made from aluminium. The Peterbilt

362 is a 40-ton truck tractor unit for highway use and comes with a 300-bhp Cummins diesel engine, a nine-speed transmission and Rockwell axles. A sleeper cab is incorporated in the cab over engine design. The Peterbilt 359 is a similar truck but with a cab of bonneted, or conventional, design

White

This famous American truck manufacturer was acquired by Swedish Volvo in 1981 after going into liquidation. The company still manufactures trucks as Whites at plants in Utah and Virginia using a high percentage of American proprietary components. One such is the High Cabover which is assembled with a Cummins 300 bhp diesel engine, a Fuller nine-speed gearbox and Rockwell axles. The White Conventional is a similar combination of components albeit in a bonneted cab design and with a thirteen-speed transmission.

ABOVE

This White is a 9000 Series 6x4 articulated tractor and is used for pulling a tanker trailer. It has a 90,000 lb gross combined weight which includes both tractor and trailer.

A Peterbilt (right) and a Kenworth (left) – two conventionals photographed in New Mexico. Both manufacturers are now part of the Paccar group.

CHAPTER THREE
GREAT BRITISH TRUCKS

The British call trucks lorries and in the earliest days of truck manufacture numerous companies started up in production. Methods of construction were entirely traditional with wooden-framed cabs mounted on engine-chassis. As with all developing industries, some of these pioneer companies fell by the wayside while others joined them later. World War II saw a shift in attitudes to truck building when the requirement was for large numbers of mass-produced trucks for the war effort. The arrival of U.S. trucks in Britain, designed for this purpose, pointed the way to the future when, for example, steel quickly began to replace wooden-framed cabs. In the postwar years many companies merged or were absorbed by industrial groups – a process which continues to this day.

A particularly notable journey was made by a British Army Major, Court Treatt and his companions, in two Crossley trucks. The trucks were ex-military vehicles of 25/30 hp and were extensively modified for the arduous journey. The plan was a trip from the Cape of Good Hope in South Africa to Cairo in Egypt. They left in September 1924 and after an extremely tough ride arrived in Cairo in January 1926. Some river crossings had to be negotiated by

removing the spark plugs and winding the trucks across the river beds on the starting handle allowing them to fill with water before emptying the engines and changing the oils on the far bank. They were the first to drive the Cape to Cairo route.

AEC

The Associated Engineering Company of Southall, Middlesex, England, started production in Walthamstow in 1912 with the B-type omnibus but soon diverged into truck manufacture when it supplied 1,000 Y-type models to the British Army for use in World War I. In the Thirties the company produced an eight-wheeled chassis known as the Mammoth Major and during World War II produced the AEC Matador as a gun tractor, its diesel engines being fitted to Cruiser and Valentine tanks. Shortly after the war, the company became part of Associated Commercial Vehicles Limited and its postwar range included Marshals, Mandators, Militants and Mercuries as well as the Type 690 10-cubic yard dump truck for excavation works.

Albion

Albion was a Glasgow, Scotland-based company which was founded in 1899 and produced its first commercial vehicle in 1902. This was a half-ton van

AEC – the Associated Engineering Company – built a range of truck and bus chassis to a cabover design which included the Monarch (right). It went on to build the famous AEC Matador as a 4x4 gun tractor during World War II.

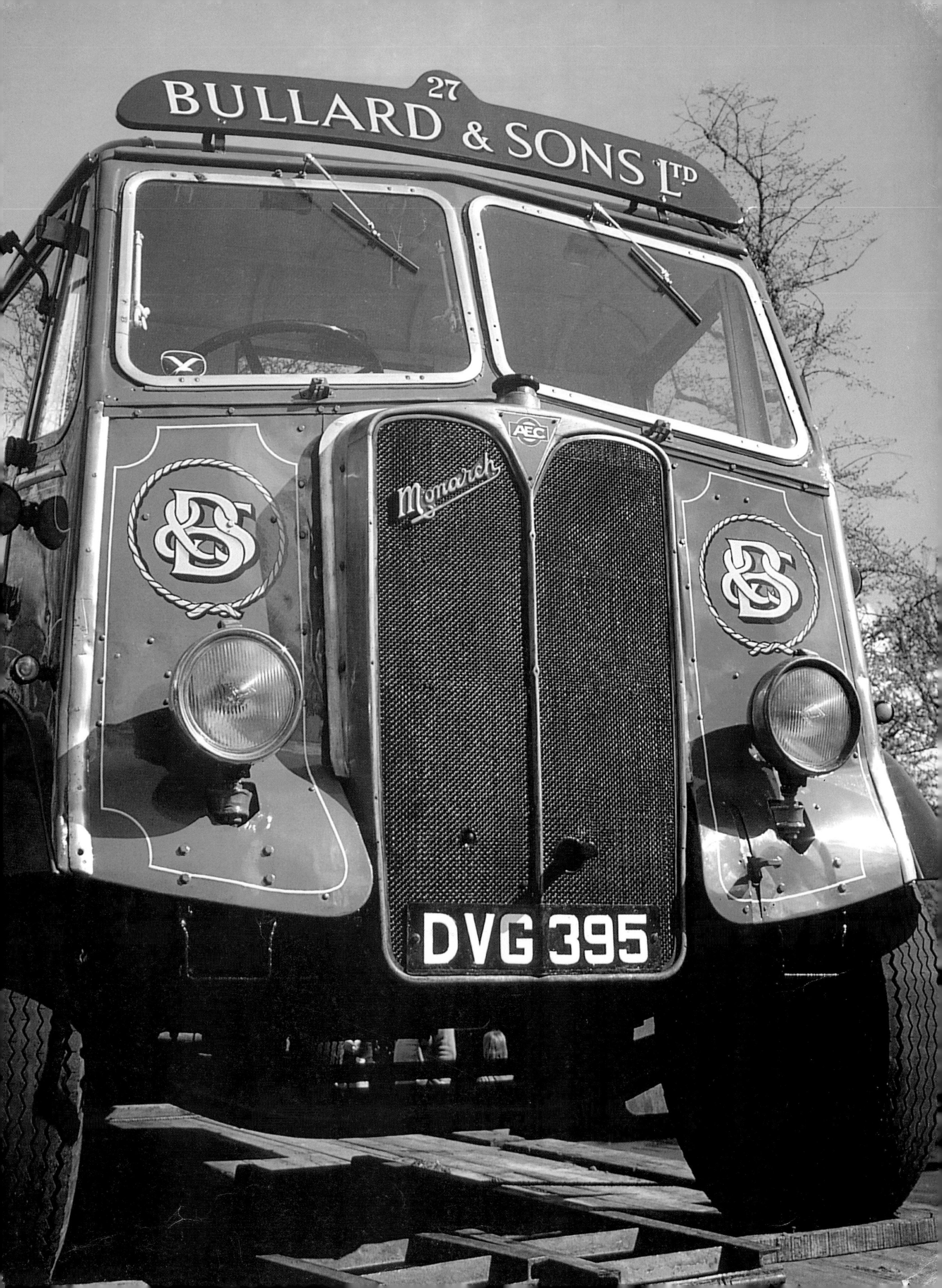
27
BULLARD & SONS LTD
AEC
Monarch
DVG 395

and was soon followed by larger vehicles prior to World War I. During the conflict, production was concentrated on a three-tonner of which 6,000 were built. The A10 was a 0.75-ton truck introduced in 1910 which survived until 1926 with only minor upgrades. The A10 featured a four-cylinder gasoline engine and a choice of either three- or four-speed transmissions. The company continued in business throughout World War II producing tank transporters, gun tractors and general purpose trucks. The first postwar Albion was the CX27, a twin steering six-wheeler of 1946. It was capable of carrying 11 tons and there was a choice of either diesel or gasoline engines. The Albion company became part of the Leyland Group in 1951 and produced Chieftain, Clydesdale and Reiver trucks throughout the Sixties. The Super Reiver 20 was a six-wheeler and was an uprated version of the mid-Sixties Super Reiver 19. The newer model was powered by a Leyland Powerplus six-cylinder diesel that produced 125 bhp driving through a five-speed constant mesh transmission to a tandem drive

spiral bevel rear bogie. It was otherwise traditional, based on a channel chassis with semi-elliptic springs and I-section front axle. Wheels were 20 inches in diameter.

Atkinson

Atkinson Vehicles Limited was founded in 1907, specialized in the repair of vehicles and began to build steam-powered vehicles in 1914. Atkinson did a lot of conversion work; upgrading solid tyred vehicles to pneumatic and petrol engines to diesel through the Twenties and building its own first diesel truck in 1933 using a Gardner engine. In the postwar years the company manufactured a range of trucks using Rolls Royce, Cummins and Gardner engines.

Austin

Austin is possibly better known as a car manufacturer although over the years it has made trucks and four-wheel-drive vehicles. The company's first commercial vehicle – a light van – was manufactured at Longbridge, Birmingham, England, in 1909. A larger truck soon followed which was unusual in that it had a propshaft to each rear wheel. Through the Twenties Austin

built a 30-cwt truck but one of their most famous trucks was the Military Ambulance of World War II along with six- and four-wheeled trucks. Commercial production continued after the war and a range of trucks was offered including 2-, 3- and 5-ton models and new models with similar payloads in the mid-Fifties. The Loadstar range was introduced in December 1949 and was heralded as something special. There was seating for three in the cab, longer leg-room for driver and crew and almost car-like styling. It was powered by a six-

cylinder gasoline engine that produced 68 bhp and drove through a four-speed transmission. The Austin Company joined the Nuffield Organization in 1952 and formed the British Motor Corporation.

Bedford

This company, which is now part of General Motors, began by assembling Chevrolet and GMC products in Hendon, England, in 1930. These were superseded in 1931 by British-built commercials although they still resembled the American vehicles. During World War II, the company

produced almost 250,000 trucks for the Allies including the 4x4 QL model which, as a chassis-cab, was the basis of a number of variants which included supply trucks, gun tractors, radio trucks and more. After the war, production of a range of proven vehicles resumed, including the 1.5-ton K-series as well as two- and five-tonners. Another range of military vehicles appeared in 1952, the R series of 4x4 trucks. These were later superseded by MK and TK models.

Commer

Commercial Cars Limited was formed in 1905 and started off by producing a

ABOVE LEFT
Another AEC, the Mammoth Major, was a four axle rigid truck built during the Thirties.

ABOVE
Seddon-Atkinson was the name given to the resultant company after the merger of the two well known British truck makers, Seddon and Atkinson, in 1970. The new company was acquired by ENASA in 1983. In 1995, the Strato 325 tractor unit was being produced by the company.

four-ton truck with iron-tyred wheels. This was followed by the SC Type of 1907 and the BC type of 1910 and soon after there were twelve trucks in the Commer range. Commer, like many British manufacturers, made trucks for the British Army during World War I and in the interwar years reverted to civilian truck production. In 1926, Humber bought the Commer concern and introduced a new range of trucks which remained in production until Rootes Securities Limited took over the company in 1928. Through the Thirties, Commer produced the Centaur and N-Series of trucks. More than 20,000 trucks rolled out of the Commer factory to help the British war effort between 1939 and 1945 before the company could once again build civilian trucks.

Daimler

Daimler, as mentioned in Chapter One, was formed in 1893 and its first British-built commercial vehicle was made in its Coventry factory in 1897. An interesting vehicle was constructed by the company in 1908 known as a road train (a name that would become more famous in Australia much later) which pulled a number of six-wheeled trailers with driven wheels. Daimler made a variety of vehicles for military purposes during World War I. The company earned a reputation for well engineered buses between the wars and for a number of armoured cars during World War II. In 1960, Daimler was taken over by Jaguar and subsequently concentrated on buses and coaches.

Dennis

Dennis made its first commercial vehicle, a box van, in 1904 and by 1908 had built its first fire engine. While it did not concentrate exclusively on fire engines from then on it was always a major part of its business. Alongside

LEFT
A 1984 Foden four-axle rigid being operated in England. Foden was acquired by Paccar, who already owned Kenworth, Peterbilt and Dart, in 1980.

ABOVE
The 1977 B-series ERF is stuck in the snow of an English winter despite a four-axle configuration.

PREVIOUS PAGE
ERF were the initials of the company's founder Eric Richard Foden who split from Foden and went on to start another truck manufacturing plant in Cheshire, England. The new company started in business in 1933 and made this three-axle rigid in 1937. It is powered by a Gardner diesel engine.

NEXT PAGE
This Leyland Constructor tipper truck is powered by a 265-horse-powered Rolls Royce engine and is available in various axel configurations.

fire appliances were made buses and trucks, the most notable of which was the Pax V Truck that featured a Perkins diesel engine. Towards the middle of the roaring Twenties Dennis introduced the 30-cwt truck with a payload of 1.5 tons which remained in production into the Thirties. Its four-cylinder gasoline engine produced 18 bhp and drove the rear axle which, like the front one, was mounted on semi-elliptic springs. Wheels by this time were fitted with pneumatic tyres.

ERF

These initials stand for Eric Richard Foden who was one of the famous Foden family of truck makers who set up on his own in the vicinity of Foden's Cheshire works. The first ERF was a Gardner diesel engine-powered truck made in 1933. Later, in the same decade, the company made six- and eight-wheeler chassis. It followed this with the first ever twin-steered six-wheeler in 1937. The company manufactured trucks during the war, including a forestry tractor. The

Sixties saw ERF using both Perkins and Cummins diesel engines.

Foden

This family company began to make steam wagons in 1856 and persevered successfully with the type until the end of the Twenties. It then switched to trucks powered by Gardner diesel engines. The R-type was introduced in 1931 and featured a five-cylinder Gardner diesel and eight-speed transmission but was otherwise traditional. The DG6-15 was a new truck for 1936 and was an eight-wheeler although later numerous variants were built. It was later superseded by the FG Series. The company made tanks for the British Army during World War II and in the postwar years made a range of trucks with a distinctive rounded cab in four-, six- and eight-wheeled configurations. The company became part of the American Paccar group in 1980. Foden also has an assembly plant in South Africa.

Guy

The first truck made by this company

in the English Midlands was a 1.5-ton model. Then, in the interwar years, it made a special cross-country truck as well as a articulated six-wheeler. Then World War II intervened and Guy manufactured military vehicles until it could start producing its postwar range in earnest. This range included the Arab, Wolf, Vixen and Otter trucks. The company was acquired by Jaguar Cars in 1961.

Karrier

Clayton and Co. (Huddersfield) Limited built the first Karrier vehicle in 1908. After spending the years of World War I building military trucks to the subsidy specification it evolved a range of municipal vehicles that included refuse trucks alongside more general purpose cargo trucks. Like the other British truck manufacturers, its production capability aided the British war effort in the manufacture of trucks and armoured cars. A postwar range of civilian vehicles included the Bantam and Gamecock models.

Leyland

This Lancashire, England-based company made its first truck, a steam-powered machine in 1896. By the beginning of the 20th century it was manufacturing trucks and buses with petrol engines. In 1904 it manufactured the Pig, a two-cylinder in-line petrol-engined truck with a 1.5-ton payload. Its transmission was three-speed and based around a bolted and riveted angle iron chassis with semi-elliptic springs and iron-shod wheels all round. The load bed was flat and the cab open. This led to large production of the 3-ton RAF Leyland that was built during World War I. Its postwar range of both buses and trucks was based on this model. The P-series of 1920 was known as the 'over-type' which simply meant that the design was of cab over

engine in order to increase the load space. The P-type featured a four-cylinder gasoline engine and four-speed sliding-mesh transmission. Otherwise it was typical of its time being based on a channel ladder chassis with semi-elliptic springs and solid-tyred wheels all round. The firm made tanks during World War II and produced an extensive postwar range of vehicles that included the Beaver,

Retriever and Octopus in the Sixties that had various chassis configurations based around a similar cab arrangement as was the Steer. The Steer was a tractor unit with a close-coupled first and second steering axle and a driven third axle. It was only produced in small numbers.

Leyland acquired Scammell which it used to produce its specialist vehicles while retaining a minority

shortlived product of the Morris company and after 1932 the firm concentrated on goods vehicles. The Morris Commercial was a common sight in the camouflage paint of the British Army during World War II although Morris also manufactured tanks. Morris, as part of the Nuffield Organization, and Austin merged in 1952 to form the British Motor Corporation and both the Austin and Morris ranges were progressively standardized. The FG Series of trucks was introduced in 1959 and later there were FJ models.

Scammell

This company, based in Watford, England, was formed in 1922 to build tractor and semi-trailer combinations. Early production was of a six-wheeler with chain drive and solid tyres that could carry 7.5 tons. The 100-tonner of 1929 was an example of this. It was a truck capable of carrying railway locomotives and built for Marston's Road Services Limited. Originally, it was equipped with a four-cylinder gasoline engine but this was replaced in the early Thirties by a Gardner diesel that made it necessary for the chassis to be lengthened. The truck was complex, its front suspension having semi-elliptic springs while its rear system was made of rocking beams. Transmission was four-speed and final-drive a combination of both prop shaft and chains through a counter shaft differential. The company experimented with heavy trucks capable of crossing difficult terrain and resulted in the Pioneer which became one of World War I's most famous British trucks. The Pioneer was built in semi-trailer guise for the transport of tanks, as a heavy recovery truck and a heavy artillery tractor. The Pioneer was powered by a 102-bhp diesel engine

shareholding in Ashok Leyland, an Indian truck manufacturer, and BMC Sanayi, a similar organization in Turkey. One of the specialist vehicles produced by Scammell is the S24 tank transporter. This huge vehicle is powered by a Cummins 320-bhp turbo-diesel driving through a fifteen-speed Fuller gearbox to six-wheel-drive axles. The tank is transported on a semi-trailer. In India, Ashok Leyland

produce the Comet, a medium-sized truck of fixed cab over engine design.

Morris

In the first decade of commercial vehicle manufacture Morris was primarily concerned with light vans which it built at Cowley, England. In 1923 the company started to manufacture the One Ton Morris and by the end of that decade was making trucks and buses. Buses were a

BELOW

The Morris Commercial was a popular medium-weight truck made by the famous English company during the Thirties. During World War II, a great many Morris Commercials were supplied to the British Army. This particular 1-ton model was used by an English brewery.

RIGHT

Scammell of Watford, England, also supplied many of its trucks to the British Army. The 6x6 Explorer was a developed version of the 6x4 Pioneer of World War II fame. The Explorer saw service in such conflicts as the Korean War. This one is taking part in a cross-country truck trial in France.

and featured a 6x4 six-speed transmission and air-assisted brakes. The Explorer, a 6x6 version of the truck was built in the Fifties as were Constructors, Contractors and Himalayans. Scammell also made an articulated tractor cab known as the Handyman and an eight-wheeler variant, the Routeman. Another side to Scammell's heavy vehicle business was that it was one of the few truck manufacturers to build vehicles especially for fairground operators, one such being the Showtrac. This tractor unit had a Gardner six-cylinder diesel 102-bhp engine and a six-speed constant mesh gearbox.

Thornycroft

This is another company whose origins were in steam-wagon manufacture. Its first was exhibited in 1896 and was soon followed by others. They were successful machines and some were

supplied to the British for use in the Boer War. In 1902 Thornycroft made its first petrol-engined truck which led it to build J-type trucks for the British Army in World War I. It continued to produce the model after the war and upgraded it by fitting a more powerful engine. At the commencement of World War II, Thornycroft was in a position to build more than 13,000 trucks and 8,000 tracked vehicles for the war effort.

In the postwar years the Mighty Antar tractor unit was developed which is powered by a 280-bhp Rolls Royce diesel engine. The Nubian 4x4 truck was frequently used as the basis for firefighting trucks as well as for tippers in major construction and excavation schemes.

CHAPTER FOUR
GREAT EUROPEAN TRUCKS

Most European countries on both sides of the former Iron Curtain produced trucks from the earliest days of its existence as a concept of division until today. Many mergers and amalgamations considerably reduced the numbers of original manufacturers, some mergers going right back to the earliest decades of this century as demonstrated by the case of Scania Vabis examined later in this chapter.

Avia

This company started as an aircraft repair company but began to make light trucks in 1957. In 1972 Motor Iberica, the makers of Ebro vehicles, acquired overall control of the company and supervised Avia's manufacture of Perkins-engined trucks and buses. One of these is the Avia 5000, the numerical suffix referring to an approximation of the truck's payload in kilograms. It is powered by an 88-bhp Perkins diesel and drives through a five-speed gearbox.

Berliet

Berliet was the surname of a Frenchman who made his first car in 1895. Subsequently a company run by Marius Berliet developed into France's largest producer of heavy vehicles. The company manufactures road-going as well as oilfield trucks. The company

was acquired by Renault in 1974 and combined with Saviem (an amalgamation of Latil, Somua and Renault's own truck producer). Since then all the commercials made by the company have been marketed as Renaults.

Büssing

Büssing is one of Germany's oldest truck makers and made its first truck around 1903. It manufactured trucks, including innovative underfloor-engined trucks and buses, from the Thirties until the Seventies. In 1971 it was acquired by MAN when its products were badged as MAN-Büssing. The 16.320U was typical of the company's post-amalgamation products, its number referring to the truck's payload. The cab over engine truck was powered by a flat-six 320-bhp underfloor diesel engine.

DAF

DAF Trucks is situated in Eindhoven, Holland. Its name originates from Van Doorne's Automobielfabrieken which was founded in 1928 to build trailers. This was followed by the manufacture, from 1949 onwards, of trucks built mainly from Leyland components. As the company became more established, however, the components of the trucks became increasingly home-produced. In 1972 International Harvester bought a

DAF is a Dutch truck manufacturer who makes machines such as this turbo-diesel 2100 model of 1988. This one is fitted with a tanker body and is being used to refuel fishing boats; but the three-axle configuration lends itself to many applications.

ABOVE

IVECO is partially owned by the Italian Fiat company and in the early Nineties produced the Turbostar. It features a high-specification sleeper cab and wind deflector on top of the cab roof.

OPPOSITE ABOVE

An older product of the Fiat factory is this 130 NC tanker photographed in Hurghada, Egypt.

OPPOSITE BELOW

Magirus Deutz makes a number of specialist trucks including this turbo-diesel 4x4 cross-country vehicle.

33 per cent interest in the company. By the mid-Eighties Daf was manufacturing around 15,000 commercial vehicles per year and employing almost 9,000 people worldwide. Daf has assembly plants in Portugal, Morocco, Zimbabwe and Australia. Nowadays, it also produces vehicles in Britain in the Leyland factory.

Ebro

Ebro was founded in 1920 to licence-build Fords in Spain. It was nationalized in 1954 when its name was changed from Ford Motor Iberica to Motor Iberica. It built trucks based on a British Ford design and named them after a major Spanish river, the Ebro. In 1971 the company acquired the makers of Siata and Avia commercial vehicles and in recent years has cooperated with Nissan to

build a variety of Japanese vehicles under licence.

Faun

Faun is a German company whose roots lie in the manufacture of steam vehicles, its first being a steam-driven fire engine made in 1890. The company's name is an acronym of Fahrzeugfabriken Ansbach und Nürnberg and it made a number of municipal vehicles and ambulances for the German Army of World War I. In the Twenties it manufactured double-decker buses and municipal vehicles which, along with firefighting vehicles and a number of specialist heavy vehicles, still form an important part of its business.

Fiat

Based in Turin, Italy, this motor manufacturer made its first truck in

1903 and its first bus in 1906. Over the years Fiat has acquired a number of other commercial vehicle manufacturers including OM in 1938, Unic in 1966 and Lancia in 1969. In 1975 KHD, manufacturers of Magirus Deutz trucks and Fiat jointly formed IVECO – an acronym for Industrial Vehicle Corporation – to coordinate development and production at its factories around Europe.

IVECO

This organization is the result of cooperation between Magirus Deutz and Fiat that was initiated in 1975. From the early Eighties, all the company's products were badged as IVECO. Ford of Britain also collaborates with IVECO.

MAN

MAN – Maschinenfabrik Augsburg

Nürnberg AG – was established as a heavy engineering works in 1840. In the 1890s Dr. Diesel worked at the factory carrying out his research into a practical engine. This ultimately led to the first MAN diesel truck of 1924. It was based on a licence-built Saurer gasoline truck that was being constructed by MAN since World War I. In 1971, MAN took over Büssing Automobilwerke. MAN cooperates closely with Saviem-Renault as well as allowing its products to be licence-built in places such as Romania where its products are badged as Roman. One such is the 1990 19.215 DFK, a 6x4 chassis fitted with a 215-bhp diesel engine. Another company with close connections to MAN is Raba of Hungary.

Magirus Deutz

The German concern, Magirus, started out by manufacturing horse-drawn fire appliances but was producing trucks by 1916. In 1938 it merged with the Humboldt-Deutz engine company to form Magirus Deutz. For the duration of World War II the company developed air-cooled engines for which it became famous in the postwar years. Magirus Deutz is currently one of the partners in IVECO.

In Slovenia TAM produced trucks that were closely related to Magirus prior to their involvement with IVECO. One such model was the T11 BK diesel. Zastava, a Yugoslavian company, has connections with Fiat and IVECO and manufactures trucks designated as 645AD and 642N

Mercedes-Benz

One of the world's major truck producers is Mercedes-Benz who in the late Eighties was producing in excess of 200,000 trucks per year. Mercedes-Benz managed to acquire the famous American manufacturer White's Freightliner range in 1981 when White was split up. Mercedes-Benz also owns Spanish Mevosa and collaborates with FAP, another Yugoslavian company. The Freightliner range of U.S. trucks and their European counterparts are distinctly different. The U.S. models are

typical of that market with both cabover and conventional designs while the European models, such as the 1320, 1638, 3850A and L1113, are conventional modern European designs.

Renault

This company is France's only major truck producer. It created Saviem from its own operation and that of Somua and Latil during the Fifties. In 1974 it acquired Berliet and has subsequently marketed all its trucks as Renaults. The company has a stake in Mack and the British and Spanish Dodge factories. The G230 and 290 trucks are built in both French and British factories.

Saurer

Saurer is an old-established Swiss company who manufactured its first car in 1896. It soon began truck production and its early models were exported and licence-produced as far away as the United States, the American factory eventually merging with Mack. Saurer was among the pioneers of diesel-engined trucks. In the late Seventies it produced the 5DF 6x2 tractor unit. This truck featured air suspension and two steering axles. Motive power came from a 11.95-litre turbo-diesel engine of Saurer's own manufacture which drives the rear axle through an eight-speed gearbox.

ABOVE LEFT

Races such as the Paris-Dakar desert 'raid' attract entries in all classes, including trucks. One competitor is this Mercedes-Benz although it is seen here supporting a team in the annual Tour de France cycle race.

RIGHT

MAN produces a range of forward control trucks that cover numerous models up to 150 tonnes gross train weight. This 1983 model is a 19.280 rigid cargo truck.

Scania-Vabis

A factory was established in Södertälje, Sweden on the Baltic coast that made wagons for the Swedish railways. The company was acquired by an iron foundry, Surahammars Bruk, in 1890 who modernized the factory and re-opened it in 1891 as Vagnfabriks Aktiebolaget i Södertälje or VABIS. The company continued in railway wagon production but was conscious that once the rail network was complete there would remain limited opportunities for it. As a result, one of its engineers, Gustaf Erikson, was despatched to Europe to see what was happening in the fledgeling motor vehicle industry. What he saw fired both his enthusiasm and his imagination and on returning he recommended that Vabis become seriously involved in the production of motorized vehicles. Erikson was concerned about the safety aspect of using gasoline as a fuel and designed

his first engines to run on kerosene. One of his earliest designs was a twin-cylinder, tiller-steered four-seater machine with additional space for goods and featured wooden wheels with iron tyres. The first truck was built by Vabis in 1903 and was designed to use gasoline as fuel, Erikson having overcome his earlier reservations. It was of advanced design with a front-mounted radiator, a 15-horse-power V-twin engine covered by a hood. Suspension was by means of semi-elliptic springs and the drive by means of a shaft to the rear axle.

Elsewhere in Sweden another industrial concern was producing a variety of products including bicycles and motorcycles. Maskinenfabrik AB Scania was the company's name and it experimented with its first car design in 1901. It manufactured its first truck in 1902 which featured chain-drive, semi-elliptic springs and wooden

spoked wheels. It was driven as a publicity stunt 650 kilometres to the 1903 Stockholm Motor Show over roads that were in execrable condition. The journey was completed in only 32 hours and brought Scania numerous accolades, including an honour from the Royal Family! Despite the two companies being effectively rivals, there was room for both of them given the size of the country and scale of truck production. But by the end of the decade the two decided to merge, the reasons being that both companies required greater production facilities and increased cost-effectiveness in order to compete with cheaper American imports. In 1911, the resultant company became Scania-Vabis Aktiebolaget. In the short term the company continued production of the Type 5 Vabis which had been proven as a reliable and durable truck.

The engineers pooled their

resources and produced a number of different engines, including some with marine and aeronautical applications as well as new designs for commercial vehicles, a new range being introduced in 1913. Exports were profitable until after World War I when the market became depressed. Neutral Sweden, however, had made provisions for its own defence and Scania-Vabis was able to supply a four-wheel-drive, four-wheel-steer truck for its soldiers as well as civilian versions which soon became popular in the timber industry. The company continued development of four-wheel-drive trucks, including fire engines, and later developed a machine designed to surface roads using hydraulic tipping gear and a spreader that could be used to lay different thicknesses of road surfacing materials. The next development was a double reduction axle that killed off chain drive in Scania-Vabis trucks and at the same time examined bus production as a feasible concept. Scania-Vabis was successful to such an extent that in some years during the Thirties bus production exceeded that of trucks.

Despite the move to the diesel engine over much of Europe, Scania-Vabis stayed with gasoline but by 1927 was forced to look at diesel as a cheaper alternative to gasoline following demands from long-distance operators. Jonas Hesselman had already patented a way of running an engine on diesel after it had been started and warmed up on gasoline. In 1930, a Hesselman-Scania type 1547 engine was offered in production trucks. It found a ready market and Scania-Vabis researched diesel engines further. In 1936 it offered its first own-design diesel engine. It was by indirect injection and an immediate success to the extent that over the next few years

the production of gasoline engines was cut by 75 per cent. The new engine provided the motive power for Scania-Vabis trucks for the next ten years although work commenced on a new range of engines in 1939. It was ten years before the new D-series engine went into mass-production. In 1951 it was made available as a turbo-diesel unit. Scania-Vabis collaborated with Leyland in Great Britain over the development of injection and cooling as well as the study of metallurgy. The Swedish company also cooperated with American truck maker Mack in the Fifties when a Mack city bus was shipped to Sweden in order that Scania-Vabis could update its bus technology: in exchange, Scania assisted Mack with their gearboxes.

Sweden remained neutral in World War II but the Swedish army purchased a number of vehicles, as it had in World War I, to continue to protect that neutrality. These were known as the SKP Armoured Truck. In the postwar years, Scania-Vabis produced the LA82 Anteater, a military cross-country truck which was a 6x6 machine and then in the early Seventies the SBAT 6x6 with automatic transmission was introduced. The six-wheeler had a 20-tonne payload and a four-wheeled version was also produced. Another feature of Scania-Vabis's business in the postwar years was increasing exports and the establishment of factories overseas. One was opened in Sao Paulo, Brazil in 1956, a plant in Tucuman in Argentina and two plants in Holland that became operational in the early Sixties.

Scania-Vabis merged with the Saab group which, in 1969, resulted in the Vabis name being dropped and the company being called AB Saab-Scania. The merger allowed for further

increases in production of the truck plants; it almost doubled from 9,610 trucks in 1970 to 18,700 in 1976.

Sisu

Sisu has been Finland's premier heavy truck builder since its foundation in 1931. In recent years it has established ties with other European truck builders and uses a number of proprietary components from manufactures such as Leyland and Rolls Royce Engines. The latter's six-cylinder engine was used in the M-162 6x2 three-axle rigid of 1978. The engine has 312 bhp and

drives the rear axle through a ten-speed gearbox. More recent Sisu trucks have been the SR series of four-axle rigids and the SM 260 CKH 6x2 tractor unit for semi-trailers.

Tatra

Tatra managed to change its nationality as a result of circumstances beyond its control; it was founded in Nesselsdorf, Moravia, then part of the Austrian crownlands, in 1897 and manufactured vehicles. In 1900 it produced the 15-hp two-ton truck that featured a two-cylinder horizontal engine fitted under

BELOW
The Tatra 815 S3 is built in the Czech Republic and features three axles, all of which are driven, and gives 6x6 capability.

LEFT
It is powered by an air-cooled V10 engine with a displacement of 15825 cc that produces 266 bhp. Transmission is five-speed but with a two-speed transfer box giving a total of ten forward and two reverse gears.

the floor at the rear of the truck. The truck was elementary and featured iron-tyred, wooden-spoked wheels. After World War I, Nesselsdorf ended up in territory administered by Czechoslovakia and the name of the town was changed to Koprivnice. From 1923 onwards the vehicles produced by the factory were called Tatras after the range of mountains. The trucks were unusual in that they featured a central backbone chassis and independent suspension at each wheel and were powered by air-cooled engines. These features are still found in Tatra products, some of which are heavy tractors and designed for off-road and military use. The Tatra T815 is a 6x6 chassis used for a number of purposes and powered by one of a choice of V8, V10 or V12 air-cooled diesel engines of up to 320 bhp.

Although changes are likely following the more liberal climate developing within Eastern Europe, truck manufacture was previously government controlled so that while Tatra concentrated on specialist and off-road trucks, Liaz, a former Soviet company, tended to build highway trucks. Some Liaz models were also built in Bulgaria badged as Madara trucks. Another Czech Republic truck maker is Avia who produce medium-capacity trucks such as the A30 fitted with a 3.6-litre four-cylinder diesel and four-speed transmission.

Volvo

Volvo's production of trucks began in 1928. It is Sweden's largest truck maker and has numerous overseas interests including factories in Australia, Britain, Belgium, Brazil, Morocco, Peru and Switzerland. Volvo acquired both White and Autocar in the U.S.A. in 1981.

ABOVE

Volvo is a renowned truck maker and produces a range of models including the FH16 of 1996 and the FL10. The F in the designation indicates that the truck is a forward control or cabover type.

RIGHT

The FL10 tipper is powered by a 299-bhp six-cylinder diesel and is available in a range of axle configurations.

CHAPTER FIVE
TRUCKS FROM AROUND THE WORLD

Hino

Hino is based in Tokyo, Japan and its origins go back to 1917. It was acquired by Toyota, another major Japanese manufacturer, and now makes medium and heavy trucks as well as a range of specialist vehicles such as dump trucks, crane chassis and fire appliances. Hino is one of the world's largest producers of trucks with assembly plants in 36 countries. One of its conventional models is the Hino NZ which is available as both 4x4 and 4x2 variants. It is fitted with a 9.4-litre 215-bhp diesel engine and six-speed gearbox. On the 4x4 model a two-speed transfer box is used. The Hino SH Series are tractor units for semi-trailers and come with a variety of options; engines range from 260- to 320-bhp diesels and six- and nine-speed gearboxes are available. The three-axle models are known as the SS Series.

Indian Trucks

India has numerous manufacturers of motor vehicles, many of which are based on original designs from other countries. This also applies to trucks, the Hindustan J6 being based on a Fifties design from British Bedford. It has a 5.4-litre 112-bhp diesel engine and four- or five-speed gearbox. The idea of utilizing older designs is not restricted to India as a similar type of truck is built in Turkey by Genoto. Another Indian truck maker is Tata whose products are styled on Mercedes-Benz designs. The PPTW-1312 truck is a cabover design of medium-weight while the company also produces bonneted designs in both 4x2 and 4x4 configurations. A third Indian manufacturers is Premier who make the Perkins-engined Roadmaster, the PFR 122SF. Other Indian truck makers are Ashok and Shakti who have connections with Leyland and MAN respectively.

Isuzu

This is another Tokyo-based concern that has links with General Motors. The company began to make cars in 1916 and later made British Wolseley cars and trucks under licence between 1918 and 1927. The name Isuzu was adopted in 1934; by 1941 the company was making diesel-engined trucks for the Japanese Army for use in its war effort. Postwar production has concentrated on trucks and four-wheel-drive vehicles. The TWD20 is a 6x6 truck made at the end of the Seventies. It is a general purpose cargo wagon with a six-cylinder 6126-cc (374-cu in) diesel engine of 125 bhp. Transmission is by means of a four-speed gearbox and two-speed transfer box.

A 1974 Isuzu TX photographed in Tanzania, Africa. The TX is intended for loads of up to 6.5 tons and was also available in a cab over engine design as well as the bonneted type seen here.

Leader

This Australian manufacturer produces
trucks in Toowoomba, Australia, which
are of both cabover and conventional
designs and feature a number of
proprietary components. The four-axle
A8 208 Mid-Ranger of 1978 features a
Caterpillar V8 diesel that displaces 10.4
litres and develops 200 bhp. A choice
of either four-speed automatic, five-
speed automatic and thirteen-speed
manual transmissions was made

ABOVE

Leader trucks are manufactured in
Queensland, Australia and features this
Sundowner sleeper cabin in its range.
The Sundowner is sold powered by a
Caterpillar diesel engine with the
option of a GM engine. This is a cabover
but conventional models are also
available.

OPPOSITE

Also built in Australia are International
trucks including the ACCO-C Series 1900
seen here with a tipper body. There are
seven models in the range that include
four 4x2s, a 4x4, a 6x2 and a 6x4.

available using units from Fuller and Allison. The truck is of a cab over engine design and is used in tandem with a twin axle drawbar trailer. Another of the company's four-axle trucks was the A8 406 Overlander. This featured a 217-inch wheelbase and used Rockwell axles. The chassis is made from cold rolled high tensile steel and fitted with a Caterpillar 3406 turbo-diesel engine of 14.61 litres (893 cu in) displacement which produces 325 bhp at 2100 rpm. It is connected to either a 1200 Series Roadranger or Spicer transmission and a Spicer twin plate clutch. An option was the fitment of an Allison HT750 automatic gearbox. Air brakes and power steering complete the running gear. The cab is made from reinforced fibreglass to a cabover design that is equipped with a driver's seat with suspension, a laminated windscreen and a comprehensive array of instruments to enable the operator to ensure everything works as it should. Based around a similar design of cab is the Leader Sundowner but it is extended rearwards to make it a sleeper cab. The Sundowner is intended as a tractor unit for semi-trailers and is available with a range of engines. The Caterpillar 3208 comes as standard in Mid-Ranger models and a Caterpillar 3306 in Overlanders but options of 3406 Caterpillar or various GM diesels are available to suit operators' requirements.

Mitsubishi

The logo of this Japanese company features three diamonds arranged in a triangular pattern because the name Mitsubishi translates into English as Three Diamonds. The company began in shipping and other heavy industry in the 19th century and had manufactured its first car by 1917. In 1935 it produced Japan's first

diesel commercials and so began a success story. The motor division of Mitsubishi became independent in 1970 and manufactures trucks under the brand name of Fuso.

Nissan

This is another Japanese manufacturer which produces both trucks and cars as well as light commercials such as vans. The truck producer is known as Nissan UD and manufactures medium-weight trucks such as the CMA and CMD range. These are six-cylinder diesel-powered 150-bhp cabover trucks with tilt cabs. The CWA is a larger truck with three axles and a 6x4 drive

configuration. It is powered by a 275-bhp turbo-diesel engine. Nissan has controlled Ebro in Spain since 1981.

Ramirez

This relatively small company has its base in Monterrey, Mexico and started out as a trailer manufacturer. It expanded into truck manufacture using a number of American proprietary components. The Ramirez R20 of 1978 was a semi-trailer tractor of conventional design powered by a Mexican-built Cummins six-cylinder diesel, Fuller gearbox and Eaton rear axle. Its cab was manufactured in Mexico from fibreglass. The R22 is a

ABOVE
Japan exports its products, including trucks, worldwide. Nissan, for example, has a division called Nissan UD which produces trucks and also controls Ebro in Spain. Mitsubishi produces a wide range of trucks including general cargo and specialized trucks such as cranes. This truck was photographed in Dubai, U.A.E.

RIGHT
This bus is pictured in Tanzania, Africa and is based on a Leyland truck chassis.

more recent truck from the company and can be ordered fitted with either Cummins or Detroit diesel engines, Spicer gearbox and Hendrickson tandem axle.

RFW

RFW is based in New South Wales, Australia. It was founded in 1969 and is locally owned. Its first truck was a four-axle tipper with some proprietary parts, including a Scania engine and a Bedford cab. From this, it progressed to cabs of its own design built to suit the specific needs of the specialist trucks it manufactures. One specialist truck was the RFW 6x6 fire tender which was powered by a 420 bhp diesel, a five-speed automatic transmission and permanent six-wheel drive through inter-axle differentials.

TZ 35843

LEYLAND

CHAPTER SIX
MILITARY TRUCKS

Large organizations such as armies could not operate without trucks, such is the scale of the logistics of supply in a modern army, especially when modern tactics require the utmost efficiency of mobility. One of the first major military trucking operations was called the Red Ball Express which took place during the liberation of Europe in 1944 (*See page 71 et seq*). Armies use a variety of trucks ranging from civilian commercial types which are put to military applications in almost standard form, particularly in rear echelon areas. They also utilize commercially designed cross-country vehicles that can be used for specific military purposes or easily adapted to suit specialist military roles. The third group of trucks used by armies are special vehicles designed to fulfil a specific requirement such as transporting missiles; but even some of these are based on commercial chassis.

The earliest military trucks were steam-powered gun tractors. In the case of the British Army, the Corps of Engineers acquired their first steam traction engine – known as the steam sapper – in 1868 and a second in 1872. The second of these, an Aveling and Porter, was the first mechanical transport used by the British Army in active service when it was used in the Ashanti War of 1873-74. During the Franco-Prussian War, the German Army used a pair of Fowler steam traction engines and in 1878 the Russian Army used twelve steam traction engines in the Russo-Turkish War. It was during the second Boer War in South Africa, between 1899 and 1902, that the British most successfully employed mechanical transport. The Army had in excess of 24 vehicles including an armoured traction engine and gained much useful experience in the deployment of mechanical transport. From 1910 onwards, the military authorities of most European nations began to assess the role of trucks and tractors in future conflicts. This led to the various subsidy schemes described elsewhere in this book.

At the outbreak of war in 1914, the British Expeditionary Force took approximately 1,200 vehicles with them to France, the majority of these being impressed through the subsidy scheme. The French also used trucks and buses for military duties as did the Germans who also had especially designed and constructed gun tractors, unlike the British, who were still using civilian-type steam traction engines. The United States entered the war in

The Austin 3-ton 6x4 range first saw service with the British Army in 1939. The breakdown gantry truck (right) was introduced in 1944 on a proven chassis. The body supported the gantry which could be used for lifting engines and similar objects in the field.

1917 and started work on a standardized truck referred to as the 'liberty' in an attempt to reduce the numbers of varying spare parts that had to be stocked. However, the standardized truck was slow in coming and a variety of trucks ended up being used. Once the idea had been conceived it was later to be fully implemented by the Americans. The Italians had developed a range of military vehicles which were supplied to the British and both the British and Americans supplied the Russians.

At the end of the war it was realized that the standardization of spare parts would have to be given top priority. This, however, was tempered by a reluctance to countenance the possibility of another major war, with the result that vehicular development was limited. Some new designs did surface, however. Renault in France built lightweight six-wheelers, and Citroën-Kégresse developed light half-tracks based on commercially available truck chassis. In Britain, a design of six-wheeled 6x4 trucks with a dual drive rear bogie was developed and some 4x4 trucks. All-wheel drive was developed in numerous countries, in Italy by Pavesi, in France by Latil and Renault and in America as a development of the liberty truck. Also in America FWD developed a 4x4, the Model B, and refined it. Marmon-Herrington started all-wheel drive conversions to existing commercial trucks and experimentation went on in Holland. The developments in Holland were carried out by Van Doorne of DAF and Van der Trappen and was known as the Trado system. The system was used to convert civilian Chevrolet and Ford chassis into cross-country vehicles.

In England, in 1933, a Hungarian engineer called Nicholas Straussler

Bedford manufactured 52,245 3-ton 4x4 trucks for the British Army in World War II in a variety of body styles, including troop and cargo carriers, gun tractors and signals vans. The QL was powered by a six-in-line petrol engine that produced 72 bhp. Transmission was four-speed with a two-speed transfer box.

Diamond T built a number of tank transporter trailer prime movers for the Allies during World War II. Some were retained by the U.S. Army while others, such as this one, were used by the British Army. The truck was a 6x4 tandem-drive and had a ballast box fitted over the rear axle.

designed and built a military vehicle based on a Ford that featured four-wheel-drive and four-wheel-steering that could travel either forward or in reverse in all gears. He went on to design a number of cross-country gun tractors. Germany was hamstrung by the terms of the armistice but still experimented with a range of sophisticated military vehicles including half-tracks.

When World War II erupted, catching many nations in a state of unpreparedness, the British Army were

in possession of War Department WD six-wheelers and numbers of militarized commercials but lost a high proportion of them during the withdrawal from Dunkirk in 1940. Replacing all that lost transport became an overriding priority to the extent that volume requirements had an effect on design. Production of extant designs such as the 4x2 0.75-ton infantry truck, 1.5-ton and 3-ton 6x4 types was increased and designs for a 4x4 3-tonner were considered. The first of these was the Crossley Q-type of 1940.

The Canadian truck industry started building standardized military-pattern trucks which were subsequently supplied to both the British and Australian forces as well as to the Indian Army in smaller numbers.

The U.S. Army had considered motorized transport for its armies and had a range of payloads of trucks in the planning stage by the time of the Japanese airstrike on Pearl Harbor. The lightest was the 0.25-ton 4x4 Jeep and the next were the 0.5- and 0.75-ton 4x4s such as weapon carriers, command cars and ambulances. A 1.5-ton 4x4 range was followed by the 2.5-ton 6x6 and 6x4 ranges which were the heaviest trucks that could be mass-produced at the time given the existing auto plants. The U.S. auto industry was to produce more than 3.5 million vehicles for the war effort. A percentage of these, approximately 750,000 were supplied as lend-lease to other allied nations, including both Britain and Russia.

The Russians manufactured trucks during World War II too, the GAZ and ZIL factories being among their producers. In the aftermath of the Russian Revolution of 1917 the automotive industry within the U.S.S.R. became specialized so that each plant was given a particular type of vehicle to build and plants were given the initials of the city or town where they were situated, GAZ being Gorki Automobilni Zavod.

The German Army was initially well equipped with motorized transport although a place in military plans was reserved for horse-drawn

vehicles, particularly in a supply role. In Nazi Germany during the Thirties the network of express roads, known as *autobahnen* were constructed to bring Germany out of the Depression. (A similar scheme was in progress in the United States where freeways were under construction to improve communication and help America get back to work. Coincidentally, this was the foundation for interstate trucking). The *autobahnen* enabled swift movement of troops around the country by motor vehicle and the German motor industry was also designing and testing a sophisticated range of cross-country trucks. By the late Thirties a standardized range had been designed known as *einheitstypen* (standard types), intended to replace the militarized civilian types in use up to that point. The new generation consisted of a range of military passenger cars, a range of diesel-engined trucks and a range of heavy half-tracks known as *zugkraftwagen*. They were further designated as either Kfz motor vehicle or Sd.Kfz special motor vehicle. Each vehicle type was then given a numerical suffix in order to precisely identify it. Unlike the far more standardized American trucks, spares supply was to prove difficult, particularly when the fortunes of war began to turn against the Nazis. Many of the heavier trucks were based around Mercedes-Benz and Steyr trucks, an example of the latter being the 1500A. The 4x2 trucks included such machines as the Opel Blitz as well as trucks from Borgward, Daimler-Benz and Magirus. The Germans also turned truck plants in occupied countries over to production for the Wehrmacht building both the factory's own designs or especially designed machines. The other combatant nations of World War II, the Japanese and the Italians, had

their own military vehicles, too. The Italians had, in the main, Thirties-pattern vehicles and the Japanese a range of trucks based on American vehicles, including an amphibious Toyota truck with a two-ton payload. The reason many of the Japanese vehicles were based on American types was that prior to the war certain of the U.S. manufacturers, including Chevrolet, had plants in Japan.

In the aftermath of World War II there were plenty of surplus vehicles in existence to transport the victorious allied armies and to equip other

nations, such as Israel. The Americans began to develop a new range of military trucks and eventually settled on a range of just six different chassis – all with an M prefix. The six chassis would cover vehicles from 0.25- to 10-tons reducing the spares problem further from the 18 chassis of World War II. The new range of trucks soon saw service in the Korean War. The British, too, brought out a new generation of military vehicles, some of which were used in Korea. Scammell, for example, produced a 6x6 version of the 6x4 Pioneer which was known as

The Mack NO was a prime mover for heavy artillery such as the 155mm gun. The 7.5-ton truck became known as Super Mack. The NO was introduced in 1941 and featured a special attachment to couple the gun and also a crane to lift and lower the gun trails. The winch fitted on the front bumper had a 40,000-lb pull capability.

the Explorer. It was a similar story around Europe with companies such as DAF, FN, Volvo, Fiat, MAN, Nissan and Toyota introducing military vehicles. As the years have passed, newer generations of military vehicles have been introduced and subsequently superseded.

The Red Ball Express

A trucking operation of considerable magnitude faced the allied armies after D-Day and the beginnings of the liberation of Europe. In the wake of the battle for Normandy in the summer of 1944, the size and speed of allied gains were larger than expected. If the advance was not to run out of momentum the frontline troops had to be kept sufficiently supplied. The problems inherent in this were that the allied bombing had destroyed much of the French rail network. Trucks were the only answer.

Brigadier General E.G. Plank of the U.S. Army launched the operation on 25 August 1944 under the control of two colonels. Ayers of the Motor Transport Service supervised the operation while Richmond of the Motor Transport Brigade organized the trucks and drivers. Petrol, munitions and other necessary supplies were loaded at St-Lô, France and driven to an area west of Paris to be off-loaded for the use of the fighting units. Because of the narrow French roads that were not suited to this new development in road transport, Colonels Ayers and Richmond derived a one-way system so that trucks travelled outwards on certain roads laden and returned unladen by other routes. It was not envisaged that the system would carry as much tonnage as a railway network but by running trucks 24 hours a day it was thought that the fighting troops could be kept sufficiently supplied. The nickname Red Ball Express soon stuck and before long 6,000 trucks were working the route. The majority of their loads consisted of petrol for both vehicles and aeroplanes. The liquid was carried in a variety of ways, by different types of tankers, tanker trailers and even flatbed lorries loaded with jerricans. To ensure the operation went smoothly the roads were signposted, checkpoints opened and service depots established. Civilian and non-Red Ball Express traffic was diverted to other roads. The Military Police regulated the operation and ensured that Red Ball Express trucks had priority at road junctions and the like.

The long routes took their toll of both drivers and trucks: the poorer sections of road required constant maintenance by U.S. Army engineers and trucks required frequent maintenance. They were run overloaded in order to move sufficient supplies and although at first a 25-mph speed limit was imposed this later had to be exceeded as the allied advance continued. Drivers suffered fatigue and accidents inevitably occurred: in order to keep the remainder rolling the disabled trucks were pushed off the road and recovered later. 'Keep 'em rolling' became the maxim to which the drivers worked, sweating in the cabs of 2.5-ton GMC deuce and a halfs, cabover engine Autocars and Federals and semi-trailer Chevrolets.

The allied advance went on; General Hodges took the American First Army north into Belgium and General Patton headed east with the American Third Army. This meant that the drivers of the Red Ball Express had to take their loads further to Soissons or Sommesous for the First and Third

Armies respectively. The winter of 1944 was coming on before the Allies captured the port of Antwerp and the rail system could be put back into working order to carry some of the freight. The trucking operation went on though: instead of the long journeys across France, the trucks could work from rail depots and a number of other freight routes were established as they were required. The White Ball Express moved freight from Rouen and Le

Havre, for example, and the U.S. Army truckers moved supplies up to Belgium in support of the British advances into Holland. The final major trucking operation was the XYZ Express which was instigated to establish sufficient supplies along the borders of Nazi Germany to the First, Third, Seventh and Ninth Armies on their final push into that country. Three of the stalwarts of the Red Ball Express are detailed below.

The 'deuce and a half'

One of the most famous military trucks of all time was the GMC CCKW-353 used in massive numbers by the U.S. Army in World War II and one of the stalwarts of the Red Ball Express. The CCKW-353 was one of a number of trucks built to a standardized chassis and mechanical specification for the U.S. Army but with a range of body types. There were both metal- and canvas-roofed cabs and a variety of rear body types including general cargo bodies, tippers, and van-bodied variants. There was also an amphibious version, the DUKW-353 which, because of its designation, was referred to as a 'duck'. The 2.5-ton GMC was powered by a 104-bhp in-line six-cylinder gasoline engine driving all three axles through a five-speed gearbox and two-speed transfer box. The amphibious variant used a propeller for propulsion while afloat.

Autocar U-7144T

Another stalwart of the Red Ball Express was the Autocar tractor truck. It, too, was built on a standardized 4x4 chassis and used as a tractor truck with a semi-trailer coupling on the rear of the chassis. The main producers were Autocar and White and a similar machine was also built by Federal. The Autocars towed semi-trailers that varied in the body configuration but included fuel tankers and general cargo bodies.

Diamond T 969B

In the description of the Red Ball Express, mention is made of the recovery trucks that were stationed along the routes in readiness to keep 'em rolling. One of the most famous of such wrecker trucks was the big Diamond T from the Diamond T Motor Car Company of Chicago. The company was almost exclusively the supplier of the 4-ton 6x6 chassis to the U.S. Army in a variety of configurations. In excess

of 10,000 wreckers were supplied, fitted with Holmes W-45 twin boom wrecking jibs. The massive wrecker was capable of towing most other wheeled vehicles. Its engine was a 119-bhp 8.6-litre in-line six-cylinder gasoline engine. Transmission was five-speed with a two-speed transfer case. Other variants of the Diamond T were supplied with a ballast body and were used to tow drawbar-type tank transporter trailers.

OPPOSITE
The Mack NO was powered by a six-in-line 159-bhp petrol engine that displaced 11.58 litres.

ABOVE
The Diamond T 969B wrecker of 1943 was powered by a six-in-line 119-bhp 8.6-litre engine. It was a typical application of the standardized 6x6 4-ton U.S. truck. The wrecker variant seen here is painted to identify it as working the Red Ball Express route in 1944. The twin boom W-45 wrecking equipment was supplied by Holmes.

CHAPTER SEVEN

IN CONCLUSION –
THE RACING TRUCK

The truck is truly a marvel of the 20th century but a book on the subject wouldn't be complete without mention of a fairly recent phenomenon; truck-racing. Trucks and truckers have been riding on a wave of popularity since the late Seventies when films such as *Convoy* immortalized drivers and their eighteen-wheelers on celluloid and projected them into the public eye. Citizens' Band Radio and country music are just two things that are irrevocably linked to truck-drivers and the life of the endless freeway. It was inevitable, as a result of this popularity, that someone should stumble on the idea of racing trucks. Now it is possible to see tractor units unhitched from their trailers lining up on the fire-roads of drag-strips rather than on the interstate – in the paddocks of some of the world's most famous race circuits rather than the *autobahnen*. In Europe, former motorcycle racers such as Barry Sheene and Steve Parrish have been persuaded to drive the race trucks which draw huge crowds of truckers and their families. It isn't just on circuits that trucks are raced; events such as the famous Paris-Dakar raid have a truck-racing class which has been hotly contested over the years.

Truck-driving outlaw where d'ya go?

A certain type of drag race car is classed as a 'funny car' – this is a funny truck. It is a White Freightliner powered by a rear-mounted Allison aeroplane engine from a Mustang. It is seen here wheelying down the drag-strip at Orange County, California.

TOP

Like any other circuit race, the action is close and exciting. Barry Sheene driving a DAF leads a Mercedes into a bend.

ABOVE

Harry Jansen in a Hanomag-Henschel at Donington Park, England.

RIGHT

Howard Barnes in a 1984 Scammell Roadtrain ahead of a Renault 310 – also at Donington.

Truck-racing action, clockwise from top left: A White Freightliner on the strip at Orange County; a Peterbilt conventional on the same drag-strip; the Allison aeroplane engine in Defiance, the wheely truck; and a Peterbilt, Kenworth and Freightliner in the fire-road at the drag-strip.

INDEX